# 50 South American Recipes for Home

By: Kelly Johnson

# Table of Contents

- Brazilian Feijoada
- Argentinian Asado
- Peruvian Ceviche
- Colombian Bandeja Paisa
- Chilean Empanadas
- Ecuadorian Seco de Pollo
- Uruguayan Chivito Sandwich
- Venezuelan Arepas
- Bolivian Salteñas
- Paraguayan Chipa
- Guyanese Pepperpot
- Surinamese Roti
- Brazillian Coxinha
- Colombian Ajiaco
- Peruvian Lomo Saltado
- Argentinian Humita
- Chilean Pastel de Choclo
- Ecuadorian Encebollado
- Venezuelan Pabellón Criollo
- Bolivian Silpancho
- Uruguayan Milanesa
- Guyanese Metemgee
- Paraguayan Sopa
- Brazillian Moqueca
- Peruvian Papa a la Huancaína
- Colombian Sancocho
- Argentinian Chimichurri
- Chilean Porotos Granados
- Venezuelan Hallaca
- Bolivian Saice
- Surinamese Pom
- Peruvian Anticuchos
- Brazillian Quindim
- Colombian Cazuela de Mariscos
- Uruguayan Morcilla Dulce

- Chilean Pebre
- Paraguayan Mbeju
- Ecuadorian Llapingachos
- Venezuelan Tequeños
- Bolivian Api
- Guyanese Cook-up Rice
- Peruvian Suspiro a la Limeña
- Colombian Arroz con Coco
- Argentinian Provoleta
- Chilean Humitas en Olla
- Ecuadorian Bolón de Verde
- Bolivian Llajwa
- Uruguayan Revuelto Gramajo
- Peruvian Aji de Gallina
- Brazilian Brigadeiro

**Brazilian Feijoada**

Ingredients:

For the Beans:

- 2 cups black beans, soaked overnight
- 1 onion, chopped
- 4 cloves garlic, minced
- 2 bay leaves
- Salt, to taste

For the Meat:

- 1/2 lb pork shoulder, diced
- 1/2 lb chorizo sausage, sliced
- 1/2 lb smoked sausage, sliced
- 1/2 lb bacon, chopped
- 1 smoked pork hock or pork ribs
- 1 tablespoon vegetable oil

For the Feijoada:

- 2 tablespoons vegetable oil
- 1 onion, finely chopped
- 4 cloves garlic, minced
- 2 oranges, peeled and segmented
- 2 tablespoons tomato paste
- 1 teaspoon ground cumin
- 1 teaspoon paprika
- Salt and pepper, to taste

For Serving:

- White rice
- Fresh orange slices
- Chopped fresh cilantro

Instructions:

Cook the Beans:
- In a large pot, combine the soaked black beans, chopped onion, minced garlic, bay leaves, and salt.
- Cover with water and bring to a boil. Reduce heat and simmer until beans are tender.

Prepare the Meats:
- In a separate pan, heat 1 tablespoon of vegetable oil and brown the pork shoulder, chorizo, smoked sausage, and bacon.
- Add the browned meats and smoked pork hock or ribs to the cooked beans. Simmer until meats are cooked through and flavors meld.

Make the Feijoada:
- In another pan, heat 2 tablespoons of vegetable oil and sauté chopped onions until translucent.
- Add minced garlic, tomato paste, cumin, paprika, salt, and pepper. Cook until aromatic.
- Transfer the sautéed mixture to the bean pot, stirring to combine. Simmer for an additional 15-20 minutes.

Serve:
- Remove bay leaves and any bones from the pot.
- Serve the feijoada over white rice.
- Garnish with fresh orange slices and chopped cilantro.

Enjoy:
- Feijoada is often enjoyed with traditional sides such as collard greens, farofa (toasted cassava flour), and orange slices.

This hearty and flavorful Brazilian Feijoada is a classic dish often enjoyed during festive occasions.

**Argentinian Asado**

Ingredients:

For the Marinade (Chimichurri):

- 1 cup fresh parsley, finely chopped
- 1/4 cup fresh oregano, finely chopped
- 4 cloves garlic, minced
- 1 teaspoon red pepper flakes
- 1 teaspoon salt
- 1/2 teaspoon black pepper
- 1/2 cup red wine vinegar
- 1/2 cup extra-virgin olive oil

For the Asado:

- 3-4 lbs beef ribs or flank steak
- Salt and pepper, to taste

Optional Sides:

- Salsa Criolla (Argentinian tomato and onion salsa)
- Grilled vegetables
- Chimichurri for serving

Instructions:

Prepare the Chimichurri:
- In a bowl, combine the chopped parsley, chopped oregano, minced garlic, red pepper flakes, salt, and black pepper.
- Stir in the red wine vinegar and olive oil. Mix well.
- Set aside a portion for basting during grilling, and reserve the rest for serving.

Prepare the Asado:
- If using beef ribs, separate them into individual ribs.
- Season the beef with salt and pepper on both sides.

Marinate the Meat:
- Brush the meat generously with the prepared chimichurri, covering it thoroughly.
- Allow the meat to marinate for at least 2 hours or overnight in the refrigerator.

Grill the Asado:
- Preheat the grill to medium-high heat.
- Place the marinated meat on the grill and cook to your desired level of doneness. Asado is typically served medium-rare to medium.
- Baste the meat with the reserved chimichurri during grilling for added flavor.

Rest and Serve:
- Allow the grilled meat to rest for a few minutes before serving to let the juices redistribute.
- Slice the meat and serve with additional chimichurri sauce on the side.

Optional Sides:
- Serve the Argentinian Asado with Salsa Criolla, grilled vegetables, and additional chimichurri.

Enjoy:
- Enjoy this traditional Argentinian barbecue with friends and family, accompanied by good conversation and a glass of Malbec wine.

**Peruvian Ceviche**

Ingredients:

- 1 lb fresh white fish fillets (such as sea bass or flounder), cut into bite-sized pieces
- 1 cup fresh lime juice (about 8-10 limes)
- 1 red onion, thinly sliced
- 1-2 hot peppers (aji amarillo or jalapeño), finely chopped
- 1-2 cloves garlic, minced
- 1 bunch cilantro, chopped
- 1 sweet potato, boiled and sliced
- 1 ear of corn, boiled and kernels removed
- Salt and pepper, to taste
- Ice cubes (optional)

Instructions:

Prepare the Fish:
- Place the fish pieces in a large bowl.

Lime Juice Marinade:
- Pour fresh lime juice over the fish, making sure it is completely submerged. Let it marinate in the lime juice for about 15-20 minutes. The lime juice will "cook" the fish.

Prepare Vegetables:
- While the fish is marinating, thinly slice the red onion, finely chop the hot peppers, mince the garlic, and chop the cilantro.

Assemble the Ceviche:
- Drain most of the lime juice from the fish, leaving just a little to keep the ceviche moist.
- Add the sliced red onion, chopped hot peppers, minced garlic, and chopped cilantro to the fish. Mix gently.

Season:
- Season the ceviche with salt and pepper to taste. Adjust the spice level by adding more chopped hot peppers if desired.

Chill:
- Cover the ceviche and refrigerate for at least 30 minutes to allow the flavors to meld. You can also add a few ice cubes to keep it cold.

Serve:
- Serve the Peruvian ceviche in individual bowls, garnished with slices of boiled sweet potato and kernels of boiled corn.

Enjoy:
- Enjoy this refreshing and flavorful Peruvian ceviche as a light and delicious appetizer or main dish. Serve with additional lime wedges on the side if desired.

**Colombian Bandeja Paisa**

Ingredients:

For the Red Beans:

- 1 cup dried red beans
- 6 cups water
- Salt, to taste

For the Colombian Rice:

- 2 cups white rice
- 4 cups water
- Salt, to taste

For the Carne Asada:

- 1 lb flank steak or sirloin, thinly sliced
- 2 cloves garlic, minced
- 1 teaspoon ground cumin
- 1 teaspoon paprika
- Salt and pepper, to taste
- 2 tablespoons vegetable oil

For the Chicharrón (Pork Cracklings):

- 1 cup pork belly, thinly sliced
- Salt, to taste
- Vegetable oil for frying

For the Colombian Pico de Gallo:

- 1 large tomato, diced
- 1 small red onion, finely chopped
- 1/4 cup fresh cilantro, chopped
- 1 tablespoon lime juice

- Salt and pepper, to taste

Additional Components:

- 4 fried eggs
- 4 ripe plantains, fried
- Avocado slices
- Arepas (Colombian corn cakes)

Instructions:

Red Beans:

> Rinse the red beans under cold water. In a pot, combine the red beans, water, and salt. Bring to a boil, then reduce heat and simmer until beans are tender.

Colombian Rice:

> Rinse the rice under cold water. In a pot, combine the rice, water, and salt. Bring to a boil, then reduce heat, cover, and simmer until rice is cooked.

Carne Asada:

> In a bowl, mix the sliced steak with minced garlic, ground cumin, paprika, salt, and pepper. Let it marinate for at least 30 minutes.
> Heat vegetable oil in a skillet over medium-high heat. Cook the marinated steak slices until browned and cooked through.

Chicharrón (Pork Cracklings):

> Season the pork belly slices with salt.
> In a separate pan, heat vegetable oil over medium-high heat. Fry the pork belly slices until crispy.

Colombian Pico de Gallo:

In a bowl, combine diced tomato, chopped red onion, cilantro, lime juice, salt, and pepper. Mix well.

Assembling Bandeja Paisa:

On a large serving platter, arrange portions of red beans, Colombian rice, carne asada, chicharrón, Colombian pico de gallo, fried eggs, ripe plantains, avocado slices, and arepas.
Serve immediately and enjoy this hearty and iconic Colombian dish!

Note: Bandeja Paisa is a substantial dish, so feel free to adjust the quantities based on your preferences and the number of servings needed.

**Chilean Empanadas**

*For the Dough:*

Ingredients:

- 4 cups all-purpose flour
- 1/2 cup unsalted butter, chilled and diced
- 1/2 cup lard or vegetable shortening, chilled
- 1 teaspoon salt
- 1 cup cold water

Instructions:

> In a large bowl, combine the flour and salt.
> Add the chilled diced butter and lard/shortening to the flour mixture.
> Use your fingers or a pastry cutter to work the fats into the flour until the mixture resembles coarse crumbs.
> Gradually add cold water and knead the dough until it comes together.
> Form the dough into a ball, cover it with plastic wrap, and refrigerate for at least 30 minutes.

*For the Filling:*

Ingredients:

- 1 lb ground beef
- 1 large onion, finely chopped
- 2 hard-boiled eggs, chopped
- 1 cup black olives, pitted and chopped
- 1 teaspoon ground cumin
- 1 teaspoon paprika
- Salt and pepper, to taste
- 2 tablespoons vegetable oil

Instructions:

> In a pan, heat vegetable oil over medium heat. Add chopped onions and cook until softened.
> Add ground beef to the onions and cook until browned.

Stir in ground cumin, paprika, salt, and pepper. Cook for an additional 2-3 minutes.
Remove the pan from heat and let the meat mixture cool.
Once cooled, mix in the chopped hard-boiled eggs and black olives.

*Assembly and Baking:*

Preheat your oven to 375°F (190°C).
Roll out the chilled dough on a floured surface to a thickness of about 1/8 inch.
Cut out circles (about 6-8 inches in diameter) using a round cutter or a bowl.
Place a spoonful of the meat filling in the center of each dough circle.
Fold the dough over the filling, creating a half-moon shape. Seal the edges by crimping with a fork or twisting.
Place the assembled empanadas on a baking sheet lined with parchment paper.
Beat an egg and brush it over the empanadas for a golden finish.
Bake in the preheated oven for about 20-25 minutes or until the empanadas are golden brown.

Enjoy your Chilean empanadas! Serve them warm as a delicious snack or appetizer.

**Ecuadorian Seco de Pollo**

Ingredients:

*For the Chicken Marinade:*

- 2 lbs chicken pieces (thighs, drumsticks)
- 1 onion, finely chopped
- 4 garlic cloves, minced
- 1 tablespoon ground cumin
- 1 tablespoon achiote (annatto) powder
- Salt and pepper, to taste
- Juice of 2 limes

*For the Seco de Pollo:*

- 2 tablespoons vegetable oil
- 1 red onion, finely chopped
- 2 tomatoes, diced
- 1 green bell pepper, diced
- 3 tablespoons fresh cilantro, chopped
- 2 tablespoons achiote (annatto) paste dissolved in 1/4 cup water
- 1 cup beer (light beer or Pilsner)
- 1 cup chicken broth
- 2 cups cooked hominy or corn kernels
- 2 cups potatoes, peeled and diced
- Salt and pepper, to taste
- Fresh cilantro for garnish
- Rice for serving

Instructions:

*Chicken Marinade:*

In a large bowl, combine the chicken pieces with chopped onion, minced garlic, ground cumin, achiote powder, salt, pepper, and lime juice.

Massage the marinade into the chicken, cover, and refrigerate for at least 1-2 hours or overnight for better flavor absorption.

*Seco de Pollo:*

In a large pot or Dutch oven, heat vegetable oil over medium heat.
Add the marinated chicken and brown on all sides.
Remove the chicken and set it aside.
In the same pot, add chopped red onion, diced tomatoes, diced green bell pepper, and fresh cilantro. Sauté until the vegetables are softened.
Dissolve achiote paste in water and add it to the pot, stirring well.
Return the browned chicken to the pot.
Pour in the beer and chicken broth. Bring the mixture to a simmer.
Add cooked hominy or corn kernels and diced potatoes.
Season with salt and pepper to taste.
Cover the pot and let it simmer over low heat until the chicken is cooked through and the potatoes are tender, about 30-40 minutes.
Garnish with fresh cilantro.

*To Serve:*

Serve the Seco de Pollo over rice. Enjoy this Ecuadorian dish with a side of avocado slices or a simple salad.

**Uruguayan Chivito Sandwich**

Ingredients:

*For the Chivito:*

- 1 lb beef steak (sirloin or ribeye), thinly sliced
- Salt and pepper, to taste
- 4 slices ham
- 4 slices cooked bacon
- 4 slices mozzarella cheese
- 4 large eggs
- 4 sandwich rolls or baguettes, sliced
- Lettuce leaves
- Tomato slices
- Pickles or pickled vegetables, sliced
- Olives, pitted and sliced (optional)

*For the Chimichurri Sauce:*

- 1/2 cup fresh parsley, finely chopped
- 2 cloves garlic, minced
- 1 teaspoon dried oregano
- 1/2 teaspoon red pepper flakes (adjust to taste)
- 1/4 cup red wine vinegar
- 1/2 cup extra-virgin olive oil
- Salt and pepper, to taste

Instructions:

*Chivito:*

> Season the beef steak with salt and pepper.
> In a hot skillet or grill, cook the steak slices to your preferred doneness.
> Assemble each sandwich: Start with a slice of bread, add lettuce, tomato slices, cooked steak, ham, bacon, mozzarella cheese, and pickles. Top with the second slice of bread.

*Chimichurri Sauce:*

In a bowl, combine chopped parsley, minced garlic, dried oregano, red pepper flakes, red wine vinegar, and olive oil.
Whisk the ingredients together until well combined.
Season with salt and pepper to taste.

*Fried Eggs:*

In the same skillet or on a griddle, fry the eggs to your liking.

*Assembly:*

Top each assembled Chivito sandwich with a fried egg.
Drizzle chimichurri sauce over the sandwich.
Serve the Uruguayan Chivito Sandwiches hot, and optionally, garnish with olives.

Enjoy this iconic Uruguayan sandwich, rich with layers of flavor and textures! Serve with your favorite side, such as French fries or a simple salad.

**Venezuelan Arepas**

Ingredients:

*For the Arepas:*

- 2 cups pre-cooked white or yellow cornmeal (masarepa)
- 2 1/2 cups lukewarm water
- 1 teaspoon salt
- 1 tablespoon vegetable oil (for greasing hands and forming arepas)

*For the Filling (Reina Pepiada, a popular filling):*

- 2 cups shredded cooked chicken
- 1 ripe avocado, mashed
- 1/2 cup mayonnaise
- 1 tablespoon lime or lemon juice
- Salt and pepper, to taste
- Chopped cilantro (optional)

Instructions:

*Making the Arepas:*

In a mixing bowl, combine the masarepa, lukewarm water, and salt. Mix well until you get a smooth, soft dough.
Let the dough rest for about 5 minutes to allow the cornmeal to fully absorb the water.
Divide the dough into equal portions and shape them into round discs, about 3-4 inches in diameter and 1/2 inch thick.
Heat a non-stick skillet or griddle over medium heat. Lightly grease it with oil.
Cook the arepas for about 5-7 minutes on each side or until they develop a golden-brown crust.

*Making the Filling (Reina Pepiada):*

In a bowl, mix shredded cooked chicken, mashed avocado, mayonnaise, lime or lemon juice, salt, pepper, and chopped cilantro (if using).
Adjust the seasoning according to your taste.

*Assembly:*

Once the arepas are cooked and have a golden-brown crust, carefully slice them horizontally, creating a pocket without cutting them all the way through.
Stuff each arepa with a generous amount of the Reina Pepiada filling.

*Serve:*

Serve the Venezuelan Arepas warm.
Enjoy the arepas on their own or with your favorite side dishes.

Feel free to explore other fillings for your arepas, such as shredded beef, black beans, cheese, or any other combination that suits your taste. Arepas make for a versatile and delicious meal!

**Bolivian Salteñas**

Ingredients:

*For the Dough:*

- 4 cups all-purpose flour
- 1 teaspoon baking powder
- 1 teaspoon salt
- 1/2 cup unsalted butter, cold and diced
- 2/3 cup vegetable shortening or lard
- 1 cup cold water (approximately)

*For the Filling:*

- 2 tablespoons vegetable oil
- 1 onion, finely chopped
- 2 cloves garlic, minced
- 1 lb ground beef
- 1 teaspoon ground cumin
- 1 teaspoon paprika
- 1/2 teaspoon ground black pepper
- 1/2 teaspoon ground cinnamon
- 1/4 teaspoon ground cloves
- 1/4 teaspoon ground nutmeg
- 1/4 cup raisins
- 1/4 cup green olives, chopped
- 2 hard-boiled eggs, chopped
- 1/2 cup cooked potatoes, diced
- 1/4 cup peas (fresh or frozen)
- Salt to taste
- Water or beef broth (for moistening the filling)

*For Assembling and Baking:*

- 2 beaten eggs (for egg wash)
- Sesame seeds (optional, for garnish)

Instructions:

*For the Dough:*

In a large bowl, whisk together the flour, baking powder, and salt.
Add the cold diced butter and vegetable shortening. Use your fingers to rub the fats into the flour until the mixture resembles coarse crumbs.
Gradually add cold water, mixing until a soft dough forms. The dough should not be too sticky.
Knead the dough for a few minutes until smooth. Cover and let it rest for at least 30 minutes.

*For the Filling:*

In a pan, heat vegetable oil over medium heat. Sauté chopped onions and minced garlic until softened.
Add ground beef and cook until browned.
Add ground cumin, paprika, black pepper, cinnamon, cloves, and nutmeg. Mix well.
Stir in raisins, chopped olives, chopped hard-boiled eggs, diced cooked potatoes, and peas. Add salt to taste.
Add a little water or beef broth to moisten the filling. Simmer for a few minutes until the flavors meld. The filling should be moist but not too runny.

*Assembling and Baking:*

Preheat your oven to 375°F (190°C).
Take a portion of the dough and roll it into a ball. Flatten it into a disc about 5 inches in diameter.
Place a generous spoonful of the filling in the center of the dough disc.
Fold the dough over the filling, creating a half-moon shape. Seal the edges by pinching and twisting.
Place the assembled salteñas on a baking sheet lined with parchment paper.
Beat the eggs and brush the tops of the salteñas with the egg wash.
Optionally, sprinkle sesame seeds on top for garnish.
Bake in the preheated oven for about 20-25 minutes or until the salteñas are golden brown.

Enjoy these delicious Bolivian Salteñas, a savory and flavorful pastry!

**Paraguayan Chipa**

Ingredients:

- 4 cups tapioca flour (yuca or manioc flour)
- 2 cups grated Parmesan cheese
- 2 cups grated mild white cheese (such as mozzarella)
- 1 cup unsalted butter, softened
- 4 large eggs
- 1 cup whole milk
- 1 teaspoon salt (adjust to taste)
- 1 teaspoon anise seeds (optional)
- 1 egg, beaten (for egg wash)

Instructions:

Preheat your oven to 375°F (190°C). Line baking sheets with parchment paper.
In a large mixing bowl, combine the tapioca flour, grated Parmesan cheese, grated white cheese, and salt. Mix well.
In a saucepan, heat the milk and butter over medium heat until the butter is melted. Remove from heat and let it cool slightly.
Add the eggs to the tapioca flour mixture and mix well.
Gradually add the warm milk and butter mixture to the bowl, stirring continuously until a dough forms. The dough should be soft and slightly sticky.
If using anise seeds, add them to the dough and mix well.
Allow the dough to rest for about 10-15 minutes to firm up slightly.
With lightly oiled hands, take portions of the dough and shape them into small balls or discs.
Place the shaped chipa on the prepared baking sheets, leaving some space between each.
Brush the top of each chipa with beaten egg for a shiny finish.
Bake in the preheated oven for about 15-20 minutes or until the chipa is golden brown.
Remove from the oven and let the chipa cool slightly before serving.

Enjoy these cheesy and flavorful Paraguayan Chipa as a snack or side dish! They are best when served warm.

**Guyanese Pepperpot**

Ingredients:

- 3 lbs beef, cut into chunks (traditionally, lean beef, or a mix of beef and pork is used)
- 1 cup cassareep (cassava-based sauce, available in Caribbean markets)
- 2-3 cinnamon sticks
- 6-8 cloves
- 6-8 allspice berries
- 1 tablespoon brown sugar
- 2-3 hot pepper (Scotch bonnet or habanero), whole
- 2 large onions, chopped
- 4 cloves garlic, minced
- 2 inches ginger, grated
- Salt, to taste
- 6 cups water (or as needed)
- 1 tablespoon vegetable oil

Instructions:

Prepare the Meat:
- Wash the beef chunks and pat them dry. Season with salt and set aside.

Brown the Meat:
- In a large pot, heat vegetable oil over medium-high heat.
- Brown the meat chunks in batches to get a nice sear on all sides. Remove each batch and set aside.

Aromatics and Spices:
- In the same pot, add chopped onions, minced garlic, and grated ginger. Sauté until the onions are softened.
- Add cinnamon sticks, cloves, allspice berries, and whole hot peppers. Stir to combine.

Combine Meat and Cassareep:
- Return the browned meat to the pot.
- Pour in the cassareep, ensuring the meat is well-coated.

Add Water:
- Pour in enough water to cover the meat. Adjust the quantity based on the desired thickness of the pepperpot.

Simmer and Season:
- Bring the mixture to a boil, then reduce heat to a simmer.
- Add brown sugar and additional salt if needed.
- Cover the pot and let it simmer for 2-3 hours, or until the meat is tender and the flavors have melded. Stir occasionally.

Serve:
- Pepperpot is traditionally served with bread or rice. Some also enjoy it with cassava bread.

Optional:
- For an authentic touch, it is common to let the pepperpot sit overnight and reheat the next day, allowing the flavors to intensify.

Guyanese Pepperpot is a hearty and flavorful dish, perfect for special occasions and celebrations. Enjoy the rich taste of cassareep and aromatic spices!

**Surinamese Roti**

Ingredients:

*For the Roti Dough:*

- 4 cups all-purpose flour
- 1 teaspoon baking powder
- 1 teaspoon salt
- Water, as needed

*For the Roti Filling:*

- 1 lb boneless chicken, lamb, or goat, cut into chunks
- 3 medium potatoes, peeled and cut into chunks
- 1 cup chopped green beans
- 1 cup chopped carrots
- 1 large onion, finely chopped
- 3 cloves garlic, minced
- 1 teaspoon ground cumin
- 1 teaspoon ground coriander
- 1 teaspoon ground turmeric
- 1 teaspoon garam masala
- 1 teaspoon chili powder (adjust to taste)
- Salt and pepper, to taste
- 2 tablespoons vegetable oil
- Water, as needed

*For Serving:*

- Roti bread (store-bought or homemade)
- Hard-boiled eggs, halved
- Mango chutney (optional)
- Hot sauce or sambal (optional)

Instructions:

*Roti Dough:*

In a large bowl, combine the all-purpose flour, baking powder, and salt.
Gradually add water and knead to form a smooth, elastic dough. The consistency should be soft but not sticky.
Divide the dough into golf ball-sized portions.
Roll each portion into a thin, round roti bread. You can use a rolling pin for this.

*Roti Filling:*

In a large pot, heat vegetable oil over medium heat.
Add chopped onions and minced garlic. Sauté until the onions are softened.
Add the chicken (or lamb/goat) chunks and brown them on all sides.
Stir in ground cumin, ground coriander, ground turmeric, garam masala, chili powder, salt, and pepper. Mix well.
Add chopped potatoes, green beans, and carrots to the pot. Stir to coat the vegetables and meat with the spices.
Pour in enough water to cover the ingredients. Cover the pot and let it simmer until the meat is tender, and the vegetables are cooked through. Add more water if needed to create a thick, stew-like consistency.

*Assembling:*

Serve the roti filling over the cooked roti bread.
Garnish with halved hard-boiled eggs.
Optionally, serve with mango chutney and hot sauce or sambal for extra flavor.

Enjoy your Surinamese Roti, a delicious and satisfying dish with a unique blend of flavors!

**Brazillian Coxinha**

Ingredients:

*For the Chicken Filling:*

- 2 cups shredded cooked chicken
- 1 tablespoon vegetable oil
- 1 onion, finely chopped
- 2 cloves garlic, minced
- 1 tablespoon tomato paste
- 1 cup chicken broth
- Salt and pepper, to taste
- 1 tablespoon chopped fresh cilantro (optional)

*For the Dough:*

- 2 cups chicken broth
- 2 tablespoons unsalted butter
- 2 cups all-purpose flour
- 1 teaspoon salt

*For Assembling and Frying:*

- Vegetable oil, for frying
- 2 cups breadcrumbs
- 2 eggs, beaten

Instructions:

*Chicken Filling:*

> In a pan, heat vegetable oil over medium heat. Add chopped onions and garlic, sauté until softened.
> Add shredded cooked chicken and tomato paste. Mix well.
> Pour in chicken broth and simmer until the mixture is thickened.

Season with salt and pepper to taste. Add chopped cilantro if desired. Set aside to cool.

*Dough:*

In a saucepan, heat chicken broth and butter over medium heat until it comes to a boil.
Reduce the heat to low and gradually add the flour, stirring constantly until the mixture forms a smooth dough.
Continue to cook and stir for a few more minutes until the dough pulls away from the sides of the pan.
Remove from heat and let the dough cool for a few minutes.

*Assembling:*

Take a small portion of the dough and flatten it in the palm of your hand.
Place a spoonful of the chicken filling in the center of the dough.
Encase the filling in the dough, shaping it into a teardrop or drumstick-like form.
Repeat with the remaining dough and filling.

*Coating and Frying:*

Dip each coxinha in beaten eggs and then roll it in breadcrumbs, ensuring an even coating.
In a deep fryer or a heavy-bottomed pan, heat vegetable oil to 350°F (180°C).
Fry the coxinhas in batches until they are golden brown and crispy.
Remove them from the oil and place them on a paper towel to drain excess oil.

Serve the Brazilian Coxinhas hot as a delicious snack or appetizer. Enjoy the crispy exterior and flavorful chicken filling!

**Colombian Ajiaco**

Ingredients:

*For the Ajiaco Soup:*

- 1 lb chicken, cut into pieces (a mix of bone-in and boneless)
- 1 large onion, finely chopped
- 3 cloves garlic, minced
- 3 medium-sized potatoes, peeled and diced
- 2 ears of corn, cut into thirds
- 1 lb small yellow potatoes (papas criollas), halved
- 1 lb Yukon Gold potatoes, peeled and diced
- 1 bunch fresh cilantro, chopped
- 1 bunch green onions, chopped
- 1 teaspoon ground cumin
- 8 cups chicken broth
- Salt and pepper, to taste

*For the Guascas Sauce:*

- 1 cup fresh guascas leaves (can substitute with dried guascas)
- 1/4 cup hot water

*For Serving:*

- Avocado slices
- Capers
- Heavy cream
- White rice

Instructions:

Prepare Guascas Sauce:
- If using fresh guascas, chop them finely. If using dried guascas, rehydrate them in hot water for 10-15 minutes.
- Set aside the guascas in water.

Cook Chicken:
- In a large pot, combine chicken pieces, chopped onion, minced garlic, ground cumin, salt, and pepper.
- Add chicken broth and bring to a boil. Reduce heat and let it simmer until the chicken is cooked through.

Add Potatoes:
- Add the diced Yukon Gold potatoes and continue to simmer for about 15-20 minutes until the potatoes start to soften.

Prepare Guascas Sauce:
- Blend the rehydrated or chopped guascas with a bit of water to form a thick green sauce.
- Add this guascas sauce to the pot.

Add Other Potatoes:
- Add the small yellow potatoes and continue to simmer until all the potatoes are tender.

Corn and Cilantro:
- Add the corn pieces, fresh cilantro, and chopped green onions to the pot. Simmer for an additional 10 minutes.

Adjust Seasoning:
- Taste the soup and adjust salt and pepper according to your preference.

Serve:
- Serve the Ajiaco hot with a side of cooked white rice.
- Provide sliced avocado, capers, and heavy cream as toppings for each bowl.

Enjoy this hearty and flavorful Colombian Ajiaco soup, a classic dish that showcases the diversity of Colombian cuisine!

**Peruvian Lomo Saltado**

Ingredients:

- 1 lb beef tenderloin or sirloin, thinly sliced
- 1 red onion, thinly sliced
- 2 tomatoes, cut into wedges
- 1 yellow bell pepper, thinly sliced
- 1 green bell pepper, thinly sliced
- 3 cloves garlic, minced
- 1 tablespoon soy sauce
- 1 tablespoon red wine vinegar
- 2 tablespoons vegetable oil
- 1 teaspoon ground cumin
- 1 teaspoon paprika
- Salt and black pepper, to taste
- 1/4 cup fresh cilantro, chopped
- French fries, for serving
- Cooked white rice, for serving

Instructions:

Marinate the Beef:
- In a bowl, combine the sliced beef with soy sauce, red wine vinegar, ground cumin, paprika, salt, and black pepper. Let it marinate for at least 15-20 minutes.

Cook the French Fries:
- Prepare French fries according to your preferred method. Set aside.

Stir-Fry the Beef:
- Heat vegetable oil in a large skillet or wok over high heat.
- Add the marinated beef and stir-fry for 2-3 minutes until browned and cooked through.
- Remove the beef from the skillet and set it aside.

Sauté Vegetables:
- In the same skillet, add a bit more oil if needed. Sauté the sliced red onion, garlic, and bell peppers until they are slightly tender but still crisp.
- Add the tomato wedges and continue to sauté for an additional 1-2 minutes.

Combine and Season:
- Return the cooked beef to the skillet, tossing everything together to combine.
- Adjust the seasoning with salt, pepper, soy sauce, and red wine vinegar if needed.

Finish and Garnish:
- Stir in fresh cilantro and cook for an additional minute.
- Remove from heat.

Serve:
- Serve the Lomo Saltado hot over a bed of cooked white rice.
- Garnish with additional cilantro if desired.

Lomo Saltado is often served with a side of French fries, which can be mixed into the dish or served separately. Enjoy this delicious Peruvian stir-fry!

**Argentinian Humita**

Ingredients:

*For the Humita Filling:*

- 4 cups corn kernels (fresh or frozen)
- 1 onion, finely chopped
- 2 tablespoons vegetable oil
- 1 red bell pepper, finely chopped
- 1 teaspoon paprika
- Salt and pepper, to taste
- 1/2 cup fresh cheese (queso fresco or farmer's cheese), crumbled
- 1/4 cup fresh basil or cilantro, chopped

*For the Humita Dough:*

- 3 cups cornmeal
- 1 cup all-purpose flour
- 1 cup chicken or vegetable broth, warm
- 1 cup whole milk, warm
- 1/2 cup unsalted butter, melted
- 1 teaspoon baking powder
- Salt, to taste
- Corn husks, soaked in warm water for wrapping

Instructions:

*Humita Filling:*

> In a large pan, heat vegetable oil over medium heat.
> Add chopped onions and sauté until softened.
> Add red bell pepper and continue to sauté until the vegetables are tender.
> Add corn kernels, paprika, salt, and pepper. Cook for about 5-7 minutes until the corn is cooked and the mixture is well combined.
> Remove from heat and let it cool.

Once cooled, mix in crumbled fresh cheese and chopped basil or cilantro. Set aside.

*Humita Dough:*

In a large mixing bowl, combine cornmeal, all-purpose flour, baking powder, and salt.
Gradually add warm chicken or vegetable broth, warm whole milk, and melted butter. Mix until you have a smooth, soft dough.

*Assembling Humitas:*

Take a corn husk and place a generous amount of the humita dough in the center, spreading it out to form a rectangle.
Spoon a portion of the humita filling onto the center of the dough.
Fold the sides of the corn husk over the filling, forming a rectangular packet.
Secure the ends by folding or tying with kitchen twine.
Repeat the process with the remaining dough and filling.

*Steaming Humitas:*

Arrange the humitas in a steamer basket, making sure they are standing upright.
Steam the humitas for approximately 40-50 minutes or until the dough is cooked and has a firm texture.
Let the humitas cool for a few minutes before serving.

Serve the Argentinian Humitas warm, and enjoy the delicious blend of flavors and textures!

**Chilean Pastel de Choclo**

Ingredients:

*For the Corn Pudding (Choclo):*

- 6 ears of fresh corn, kernels removed (or 4 cups frozen corn kernels)
- 1 cup whole milk
- 2 tablespoons butter
- 1 tablespoon sugar
- Salt, to taste

*For the Filling:*

- 1 lb ground beef or a mix of beef and chicken
- 1 large onion, finely chopped
- 2 cloves garlic, minced
- 1 tablespoon vegetable oil
- 2 hard-boiled eggs, sliced
- 1 cup black olives, pitted and sliced
- 1 cup raisins
- 1 teaspoon ground cumin
- Salt and pepper, to taste

*For the Topping:*

- 1 cup mashed cooked pumpkin or butternut squash
- 2 tablespoons butter
- Salt, to taste

Instructions:

*Prepare the Corn Pudding (Choclo):*

In a blender or food processor, blend the corn kernels with milk until you get a smooth mixture.

In a large pot, melt butter over medium heat. Add the corn mixture, sugar, and salt.
Cook, stirring continuously, until the mixture thickens and has a pudding-like consistency. This can take about 15-20 minutes. Set aside.

*Prepare the Filling:*

In a skillet, heat vegetable oil over medium heat. Add chopped onions and minced garlic. Sauté until the onions are translucent.
Add the ground beef (or beef and chicken mix) and cook until browned.
Season with ground cumin, salt, and pepper. Adjust the seasoning according to your taste.
Add raisins, sliced olives, and hard-boiled egg slices. Mix well and cook for an additional 5 minutes.

*Assemble the Pastel de Choclo:*

Preheat your oven to 375°F (190°C).
In a baking dish, spread a layer of the corn pudding (choclo) to form the base.
Add the meat filling on top of the corn layer, spreading it evenly.
Arrange the remaining corn pudding over the meat filling, covering it completely.

*Prepare the Topping:*

In a separate bowl, mash the cooked pumpkin or butternut squash.
Mix in butter and season with salt to taste.
Spread the mashed pumpkin or butternut squash over the top layer of corn pudding.

*Bake the Pastel de Choclo:*

Place the baking dish in the preheated oven and bake for approximately 30-40 minutes or until the top is golden brown.

*Serve:*

Allow the Pastel de Choclo to cool for a few minutes before serving.

Slice and serve the delicious Chilean dish, savoring the layers of corn pudding, flavorful meat filling, and mashed pumpkin topping.

Enjoy this traditional Chilean comfort food!

**Ecuadorian Encebollado**

Ingredients:

- 1 lb fresh tuna, cut into chunks (can also use canned tuna)
- 1 large red onion, thinly sliced
- 4 cloves garlic, minced
- 2 tomatoes, chopped
- 2 tablespoons vegetable oil
- 2 tablespoons achiote oil (annatto-infused oil, optional)
- 4 cups fish or vegetable broth
- 2 cups water
- 1 cup yuca (cassava), peeled and diced
- 1 cup fresh tomato juice
- 1/4 cup chopped cilantro
- 2 tablespoons ground cumin
- 2 tablespoons dried oregano
- 4 tablespoons lime or bitter orange juice
- Salt and pepper, to taste
- 2 cups cooked white rice (for serving)
- Sliced green onions (for garnish)
- Sliced radishes (for garnish)
- Avocado slices (for garnish)
- Hot sauce (optional)

Instructions:

In a large pot, heat vegetable oil and achiote oil over medium heat.
Add sliced red onions and minced garlic. Sauté until the onions are softened and translucent.
Add chopped tomatoes and cook until they release their juices.
Stir in ground cumin and dried oregano, mixing well to combine the flavors.
Add the fish or vegetable broth, water, yuca, and fresh tomato juice. Bring the mixture to a boil and then reduce the heat to simmer until the yuca is tender.
Once the yuca is tender, add the tuna chunks to the pot and cook until the tuna is just cooked through. Be careful not to overcook, as tuna can become tough.
Stir in chopped cilantro, lime or bitter orange juice, salt, and pepper. Adjust the seasoning according to your taste.

Serve the encebollado hot over cooked white rice.
Garnish with sliced green onions, sliced radishes, and avocado slices.
Optionally, serve with hot sauce on the side for those who like it spicier.
Enjoy the Ecuadorian encebollado as a comforting and flavorful seafood soup!

This dish is often enjoyed with additional toppings and served with sides like tostado (toasted corn) or plantain chips.

**Venezuelan Pabellón Criollo**

Ingredients:

*For the Shredded Beef:*

- 1 lb flank steak or skirt steak
- 1 large onion, chopped
- 1 bell pepper, chopped
- 3 cloves garlic, minced
- 1 cup tomato sauce
- 1 teaspoon ground cumin
- 1 teaspoon dried oregano
- Salt and pepper, to taste
- 2 cups water

*For the Black Beans:*

- 1 cup black beans (canned or soaked and cooked)
- 1 small onion, chopped
- 2 cloves garlic, minced
- 1 bay leaf
- Salt, to taste

*For the Rice:*

- 2 cups white rice
- 4 cups water
- Salt, to taste

*For the Plantains:*

- 2 ripe plantains, peeled and sliced
- Vegetable oil, for frying

Instructions:

*Shredded Beef:*

In a large pot, combine the flank steak, chopped onion, bell pepper, minced garlic, tomato sauce, ground cumin, dried oregano, salt, and pepper.
Add water to the pot until the ingredients are covered.
Bring the mixture to a boil, then reduce the heat to simmer. Cover and cook for about 2-3 hours or until the beef is tender and easily shreds.
Shred the beef using two forks. If there's excess liquid, you can simmer uncovered until it thickens.

*Black Beans:*

In a separate pot, combine soaked and cooked black beans with chopped onion, minced garlic, bay leaf, and salt.
Simmer the beans until they are tender and flavorful. Remove the bay leaf before serving.

*Rice:*

Rinse the rice under cold water until the water runs clear.
In a pot, combine the rice, water, and salt. Bring to a boil, then reduce the heat to low, cover, and simmer until the rice is cooked.

*Plantains:*

In a skillet, heat vegetable oil over medium heat.
Fry the plantain slices until they are golden brown on both sides. Remove and place them on a paper towel to absorb excess oil.

*Assemble Pabellón Criollo:*

Serve the shredded beef, black beans, rice, and fried plantains on individual plates.
Traditionally, the components are served on the plate but not mixed. Each component is enjoyed separately, allowing for a mix of flavors in each bite.
Optionally, you can add a fried egg on top for extra richness.

Enjoy the traditional Venezuelan Pabellón Criollo, a delicious and comforting meal with a combination of flavors!

**Bolivian Silpancho**

Ingredients:

*For the Milanesa (Breaded Meat):*

- 4 thin beef steaks (sirloin or flank), pounded thinly
- Salt and pepper, to taste
- 1 cup all-purpose flour
- 2 eggs, beaten
- 2 cups breadcrumbs
- Vegetable oil, for frying

*For the Mote (Mashed Potatoes):*

- 4 large potatoes, peeled and diced
- Salt, to taste
- 1/2 cup milk
- 2 tablespoons butter

*For the Salsa (Salsa Criolla):*

- 1 large tomato, finely chopped
- 1 small red onion, finely chopped
- 1/4 cup fresh cilantro, chopped
- 1/4 cup vegetable oil
- 2 tablespoons white vinegar
- Salt and pepper, to taste

*For Assembling:*

- White rice
- Fried eggs (optional, for serving on top)
- Sliced avocado (optional, for serving on the side)
- Lime wedges

Instructions:

*Prepare the Milanesa (Breaded Meat):*

Season the beef steaks with salt and pepper.
Dredge each steak in flour, shaking off excess.
Dip the floured steaks in beaten eggs.
Coat the steaks with breadcrumbs, pressing the breadcrumbs onto the meat to ensure they adhere.
Heat vegetable oil in a large skillet over medium-high heat.
Fry the breaded steaks until golden brown on both sides. Drain on paper towels.

*Prepare the Mote (Mashed Potatoes):*

Boil the diced potatoes in salted water until tender.
Drain the potatoes and mash them with milk, butter, and salt until smooth and creamy.

*Prepare the Salsa (Salsa Criolla):*

In a bowl, combine chopped tomato, chopped red onion, chopped cilantro, vegetable oil, white vinegar, salt, and pepper. Mix well.

*Assembling Silpancho:*

Place a serving of white rice on each plate.
Top the rice with a portion of the mashed potatoes, spreading them out.
Lay a breaded steak (milanesa) on top of the mashed potatoes.
Spoon salsa criolla over the milanesa.
Optionally, serve with a fried egg on top and sliced avocado on the side.
Garnish with lime wedges for squeezing over the dish.
Serve the Silpancho hot and enjoy!

Silpancho is a delicious Bolivian dish with a combination of textures and flavors. The crispy milanesa, creamy mashed potatoes, and vibrant salsa make it a satisfying meal.

**Uruguayan Milanesa**

Ingredients:

- 4 beef or veal steaks, pounded thinly
- Salt and pepper, to taste
- 1 cup all-purpose flour
- 2 eggs, beaten
- 2 cups breadcrumbs
- Vegetable oil, for frying

Instructions:

Prepare the Steaks:
- Pound the beef or veal steaks until they are thin and even.
- Season both sides of each steak with salt and pepper.

Set Up the Breading Station:
- Place the flour in one shallow dish.
- Beat the eggs in another shallow dish.
- Place the breadcrumbs in a third shallow dish.

Bread the Steaks:
- Dredge each steak in the flour, shaking off any excess.
- Dip the floured steaks into the beaten eggs, ensuring they are well-coated.
- Coat the steaks with breadcrumbs, pressing the breadcrumbs onto the meat to adhere.

Heat the Oil:
- In a large skillet, heat vegetable oil over medium-high heat.

Fry the Milanesa:
- Fry the breaded steaks in the hot oil until they are golden brown on both sides. This usually takes about 3-4 minutes per side.

Drain and Serve:
- Once the milanesa is cooked, place it on a plate lined with paper towels to absorb any excess oil.

Serve Hot:
- Serve the Uruguayan milanesa hot, optionally with a wedge of lemon or lime on the side.

Enjoy the crispy and flavorful Uruguayan milanesa as a main dish, often accompanied by mashed potatoes, a fresh salad, or your favorite side dishes!

**Guyanese Metemgee**

Ingredients:

*For the Metemgee:*

- 1 lb salted or smoked fish (salted cod or smoked herring), soaked and flaked
- 1 lb shrimp, peeled and deveined
- 1 lb okra, chopped
- 1 medium-sized eggplant, diced
- 1 medium-sized sweet potato, peeled and diced
- 1 medium-sized yam, peeled and diced
- 1 medium-sized plantain, peeled and sliced
- 1 cup pumpkin, diced
- 1 cup cassava, peeled and diced
- 1 cup eddoes or taro root, peeled and diced
- 1 cup corn kernels
- 1 medium-sized onion, chopped
- 4 cloves garlic, minced
- 2 sprigs thyme
- 2 wiri wiri peppers or Scotch bonnet peppers, whole (adjust to taste)
- Salt, to taste
- 1 tablespoon oil

*For the Coconut Milk:*

- 1 cup grated coconut
- 2 cups warm water

Instructions:

Prepare the Coconut Milk:
- Blend the grated coconut with warm water until a thick milk forms.
- Strain the coconut milk through a fine mesh sieve or cheesecloth to extract the liquid. Set aside.

Cook the Salted/Smoked Fish:

- If using salted cod, soak it in water for a few hours or overnight to remove excess salt. If using smoked herring, soak it to reduce the smokiness.
- Boil the fish until it is tender. Flake the fish and set aside.

Prepare the Vegetables:
- In a large pot, heat oil over medium heat.
- Add chopped onions, minced garlic, and wiri wiri peppers. Sauté until the onions are translucent.

Add the Root Vegetables:
- Add sweet potato, yam, plantain, pumpkin, cassava, and eddoes/taro root to the pot. Stir well.

Coconut Milk and Simmer:
- Pour in the prepared coconut milk over the vegetables.
- Add thyme sprigs and salt to taste. Stir to combine.
- Allow the vegetables to simmer until they are almost tender.

Add Okra, Shrimp, and Corn:
- Add chopped okra, peeled and deveined shrimp, and corn kernels to the pot. Stir gently.

Add Salted/Smoked Fish:
- Add the flaked salted or smoked fish to the pot. Gently stir to incorporate.

Simmer Until Cooked:
- Let the metemgee simmer until all the vegetables are cooked through, and the flavors meld together. Adjust salt and spice levels as needed.

Serve:
- Remove the wiri wiri peppers and thyme sprigs before serving.
- Serve the Guyanese metemgee hot, traditionally with rice or bread.

Enjoy this rich and hearty Guyanese metemgee, a flavorful combination of vegetables, coconut milk, and seafood!

**Paraguayan Sopa**

Ingredients:

- 2 cups cornmeal
- 1 cup all-purpose flour
- 1 cup grated Parmesan cheese
- 1 cup diced white onion
- 1 cup diced bell peppers (red and green)
- 1 cup whole milk
- 1 cup melted butter
- 4 eggs
- 1 tablespoon baking powder
- Salt and pepper, to taste

Instructions:

Preheat your oven to 350°F (175°C). Grease a baking dish (traditionally, a clay pot is used).
In a large mixing bowl, combine the cornmeal, all-purpose flour, baking powder, and a pinch of salt and pepper.
In a separate bowl, beat the eggs and then add them to the dry mixture.
Add the grated Parmesan cheese, diced onions, and diced bell peppers to the bowl. Mix everything well.
Pour in the melted butter and whole milk. Stir until you achieve a thick, but pourable batter. Adjust consistency with more milk if needed.
Pour the batter into the greased baking dish.
Bake in the preheated oven for approximately 30-40 minutes or until the top is golden brown and a toothpick inserted into the center comes out clean.
Once baked, let it cool for a few minutes before slicing and serving.

Sopa Paraguaya is often enjoyed as a side dish with grilled meats or served with a simple salad. The combination of the cheesy, cornbread-like texture makes it a unique and flavorful addition to Paraguayan cuisine.

**Brazillian Moqueca**

Ingredients:

*For the Fish Marinade:*

- 1.5 lbs firm white fish fillets (such as snapper or cod), cut into chunks
- Juice of 1 lime
- Salt and black pepper, to taste

*For the Moqueca Base:*

- 2 tablespoons olive oil
- 1 large onion, thinly sliced
- 1 red bell pepper, thinly sliced
- 1 green bell pepper, thinly sliced
- 3 tomatoes, chopped
- 3 cloves garlic, minced
- 1 tablespoon tomato paste
- 1 can (14 oz) coconut milk
- 1 cup fish or vegetable broth
- 1 tablespoon palm oil (optional, for authenticity)
- 1 bunch fresh cilantro, chopped
- 1 bunch fresh parsley, chopped
- Salt and pepper, to taste

*For Serving:*

- Cooked white rice
- Lime wedges

Instructions:

Marinate the Fish:
- In a bowl, combine the fish chunks with lime juice, salt, and black pepper. Let it marinate for about 15-30 minutes.

Prepare the Moqueca Base:
- In a large, deep skillet or pan, heat olive oil over medium heat.
- Add sliced onions and sauté until softened.

Add Vegetables:

- Add sliced red and green bell peppers to the skillet. Cook until the peppers are slightly softened.

Stir in Aromatics:
- Add minced garlic and cook for another minute until fragrant.

Tomato Paste and Tomatoes:
- Stir in tomato paste and chopped tomatoes. Cook for a few minutes until the tomatoes start to break down.

Coconut Milk and Broth:
- Pour in coconut milk and fish or vegetable broth. Mix well.

Palm Oil (Optional):
- If using palm oil for authenticity, add it to the skillet and stir.

Seasoning:
- Season the mixture with salt and pepper to taste. Remember that the fish is already seasoned.

Cook Fish:
- Gently place the marinated fish chunks into the simmering moqueca base. Cook until the fish is opaque and cooked through.

Fresh Herbs:
- Stir in chopped cilantro and parsley. Reserve some for garnish.

Serve:
- Serve the Brazilian Moqueca hot over cooked white rice.
- Garnish with additional fresh herbs and lime wedges.

Enjoy this flavorful and aromatic Brazilian Moqueca, a dish that beautifully combines the richness of coconut milk, the freshness of herbs, and the deliciousness of seafood.

**Peruvian Papa a la Huancaína**

Ingredients:

*For the Huancaina Sauce:*

- 1 1/2 cups feta cheese, crumbled
- 1/2 cup vegetable oil
- 2 to 3 yellow chili peppers (aji amarillo), seeded and deveined, chopped
- 2 cloves garlic, minced
- 1/2 cup unsalted soda crackers or saltine crackers, crushed
- 1 cup evaporated milk
- Salt and pepper, to taste

*For the Potatoes:*

- 6 to 8 yellow or white potatoes, boiled and sliced
- 4 large lettuce leaves, for serving
- 4 hard-boiled eggs, halved
- 8 black olives, pitted
- 2 tablespoons chopped fresh parsley, for garnish

Instructions:

Prepare the Huancaina Sauce:

In a blender, combine crumbled feta cheese, vegetable oil, yellow chili peppers, minced garlic, crushed crackers, and evaporated milk.
Blend until smooth, adding more milk if needed to achieve a thick but pourable consistency.
Season with salt and pepper to taste. Blend again to incorporate the seasoning.

Assemble the Dish:

Arrange the boiled and sliced potatoes on a serving plate or individual plates.
Pour the Huancaina sauce over the potatoes, ensuring they are well-covered.
Garnish with halved hard-boiled eggs, black olives, and chopped fresh parsley.

Place lettuce leaves around the edges of the plate for added presentation. Serve the Papa a la Huancaína at room temperature or chilled.

Optional:

- Some variations include serving the dish on a bed of lettuce or garnishing with additional aji amarillo slices.

Enjoy this classic Peruvian dish, Papa a la Huancaína, with its creamy and flavorful Huancaina sauce over tender potatoes!

**Colombian Sancocho**

Ingredients:

*For the Sancocho Base:*

- 1 whole chicken, cut into pieces
- 2 tablespoons vegetable oil
- 1 large onion, finely chopped
- 3 cloves garlic, minced
- 2 scallions, chopped
- 1 bell pepper, diced
- 1 large tomato, diced
- 1 teaspoon ground cumin
- 1 teaspoon dried oregano
- 8 cups chicken broth
- Salt and pepper, to taste

*Additional Ingredients:*

- 2 large ears of corn, cut into thirds
- 2 green plantains, peeled and sliced
- 2 ripe plantains, peeled and sliced
- 1 pound yuca (cassava), peeled and cut into chunks
- 1 pound potatoes, peeled and cut into chunks
- 1 bunch fresh cilantro, chopped
- 1 lime, cut into wedges

Instructions:

Prepare the Chicken:
- Season the chicken pieces with salt and pepper.

Sear the Chicken:
- In a large pot, heat vegetable oil over medium-high heat.
- Brown the chicken pieces on all sides. Once browned, remove them from the pot and set aside.

Sauté Aromatics:

- In the same pot, add chopped onions, minced garlic, scallions, diced bell pepper, cumin, and oregano. Sauté until the vegetables are softened.

Add Tomatoes:
- Stir in the diced tomatoes and cook for a few minutes until they start to break down.

Return Chicken to Pot:
- Place the seared chicken back into the pot.

Pour Chicken Broth:
- Pour in the chicken broth, ensuring it covers the chicken.

Simmer the Base:
- Bring the mixture to a boil, then reduce the heat to low, cover, and simmer for about 30 minutes.

Add Vegetables:
- Add the sliced green plantains, ripe plantains, yuca, potatoes, and corn to the pot. Mix well.

Continue Simmering:
- Cover the pot and continue simmering for another 30-40 minutes or until the vegetables are tender.

Adjust Seasoning:
- Taste and adjust the seasoning with salt and pepper as needed.

Serve:
- Serve the Colombian Sancocho hot, garnished with chopped cilantro and lime wedges on the side.

Enjoy this hearty and comforting Colombian Sancocho, a traditional soup that brings together a variety of flavors and textures!

**Argentinian Chimichurri**

Ingredients:

- 1 cup fresh parsley, finely chopped
- 4 cloves garlic, minced
- 2 tablespoons fresh oregano, chopped (or 1 tablespoon dried oregano)
- 1 teaspoon red pepper flakes (adjust to taste)
- 2 teaspoons salt
- 1/2 teaspoon black pepper
- 1/4 teaspoon cumin
- 1/2 cup red wine vinegar
- 1/2 cup extra virgin olive oil

Instructions:

Prepare Ingredients:
- Finely chop the fresh parsley, mince the garlic, and chop the fresh oregano if using.

Combine Dry Ingredients:
- In a bowl, combine the chopped parsley, minced garlic, oregano, red pepper flakes, salt, black pepper, and cumin.

Add Wet Ingredients:
- Pour in the red wine vinegar and extra virgin olive oil.

Mix Well:
- Stir the ingredients well until everything is thoroughly combined.

Resting Time:
- Let the chimichurri sauce sit for at least 30 minutes before serving. This allows the flavors to meld together.

Adjust Seasoning:
- Taste the chimichurri and adjust the seasoning according to your preference. You can add more salt, pepper, or red pepper flakes if desired.

Serve:
- Chimichurri is traditionally served as a condiment for grilled meats. Drizzle it over steak, chicken, or grilled vegetables.

Storage:
- Store any leftover chimichurri in an airtight container in the refrigerator. It can be kept for a few days.

Tips:

- For a milder version, you can reduce the amount of red pepper flakes.
- Some variations may include adding a squeeze of lemon or lime juice for a citrusy kick.

Enjoy the vibrant and flavorful Argentinian Chimichurri as a perfect complement to your grilled meats!

**Chilean Porotos Granados**

Ingredients:

- 2 cups fresh cranberry beans or shell beans (or substitute with dried beans soaked overnight)
- 1 large onion, finely chopped
- 2 cloves garlic, minced
- 2 tablespoons vegetable oil
- 2 cups fresh corn kernels (or frozen corn)
- 2 medium-sized butternut squash, peeled and diced
- 1 cup diced tomatoes (fresh or canned)
- 1 teaspoon paprika
- 1 teaspoon cumin
- 1/2 teaspoon ground black pepper
- 1 teaspoon salt (adjust to taste)
- 1/2 cup fresh basil leaves, chopped
- 2 cups water or vegetable broth
- 1 cup diced zucchini (optional)
- 1 cup diced green beans (optional)
- 1 cup diced pumpkin (optional)
- 1 cup cooked rice (for serving)

Instructions:

Prepare the Beans:
- If using dried beans, soak them overnight. If using fresh cranberry beans, shell them and set aside.

Sauté Onion and Garlic:
- In a large pot, heat vegetable oil over medium heat. Add finely chopped onions and minced garlic. Sauté until the onions are translucent.

Add Vegetables:
- Add fresh corn kernels, diced butternut squash, diced tomatoes, paprika, cumin, black pepper, and salt. Stir well.

Add Fresh Beans:
- Add the fresh cranberry beans to the pot. If using dried beans, drain and rinse them before adding.

Pour Water or Broth:

- Pour in water or vegetable broth, ensuring it covers the vegetables and beans.

Simmer:
- Bring the mixture to a boil, then reduce the heat to simmer. Cover the pot and let it cook for about 30-40 minutes or until the beans and vegetables are tender.

Optional: Add More Vegetables:
- If using additional vegetables like zucchini, green beans, or pumpkin, add them to the pot during the last 15-20 minutes of cooking.

Finish with Basil:
- Stir in the chopped fresh basil leaves during the last few minutes of cooking.

Adjust Seasoning:
- Taste the porotos granados and adjust the seasoning if needed.

Serve:
- Serve the porotos granados hot over cooked rice.

Enjoy this traditional Chilean dish, Porotos Granados, which beautifully combines fresh beans, vegetables, and aromatic spices!

**Venezuelan Hallaca**

Ingredients:

Dough (Masa):
- Pre-cooked cornmeal (masarepa)
- Chicken or vegetable broth
- Annatto-infused oil (for color)
- Salt to taste

Filling:
- Shredded and stewed meats (commonly beef, pork, and chicken)
- Raisins
- Pitted green olives
- Capers
- Onions and bell peppers
- Various spices and seasonings

Wrapping:
- Plantain leaves, softened by briefly passing over an open flame

Instructions:

Prepare the Filling:
- Cook the meats and season them with various spices. The meats are typically shredded.
- Sauté onions and bell peppers.
- Combine the meats, sautéed vegetables, raisins, olives, and capers to create a flavorful filling.

Prepare the Dough:
- Mix the pre-cooked cornmeal with warm chicken or vegetable broth until you achieve a smooth, pliable dough.
- Add annatto-infused oil for color and salt to taste.

Assemble the Hallacas:
- Lay out a softened plantain leaf and spread a thin layer of the dough on it.
- Add a portion of the filling in the center of the dough.
- Fold the plantain leaf to encase the filling securely, forming a rectangular or square-shaped packet.
- Tie the hallaca with strings made from the plantain leaf.

Cooking:

- Hallacas are traditionally boiled or steamed until the dough is cooked and has a firm consistency.

The entire process of making hallacas is a social and cultural event, often involving friends and family members coming together to prepare these delicious and symbolic dishes during the holiday season. The exact ingredients and preparation methods may vary between regions and families, but the essence of the dish remains a cherished part of Venezuelan holiday traditions.

**Bolivian Saice**

Ingredients:

Meat:
- Beef or llama meat, cut into bite-sized pieces

Vegetables:
- Potatoes, peeled and diced
- Carrots, sliced
- Green peas
- Green beans, chopped
- Corn kernels (optional)

Aromatics and Spices:
- Onion, finely chopped
- Garlic, minced
- Aji amarillo (yellow chili pepper) or other chili peppers, finely chopped
- Cumin, oregano, and other spices to taste

Liquid:
- Beef or vegetable broth
- Water

Additional Ingredients:
- Peanuts or peanut butter (for a nutty flavor and thickening)

Instructions:

Prepare the Meat:
- In a large pot, brown the meat over medium heat with a bit of oil until it's seared on all sides.

Sauté Aromatics:
- Add chopped onions, minced garlic, and chopped chili peppers to the pot. Sauté until the onions are translucent.

Add Vegetables:
- Incorporate diced potatoes, sliced carrots, green peas, and chopped green beans (and corn kernels if using).

Seasoning:
- Season the mixture with cumin, oregano, and any other desired spices. Salt can be added to taste.

Liquid and Simmering:

- Pour in beef or vegetable broth, and add enough water to cover the ingredients. Bring the stew to a boil and then reduce the heat to simmer. Allow it to cook until the meat is tender and the vegetables are cooked through.

Peanut Addition:
- Some variations of Saice include the addition of peanuts or peanut butter to provide a nutty flavor and thicken the stew. Adjust the quantity based on personal preference.

Serve:
- Once the Saice is cooked and the flavors have melded together, it is ready to be served. It is often enjoyed with rice or other side dishes.

Keep in mind that the specific recipe may vary from one region or family to another. Bolivian cuisine is diverse, and local variations can influence the preparation of traditional dishes like Saice.

**Surinamese Pom**

Ingredients:

- 2 lbs chicken, cut into pieces
- 2 lbs pomtayer (malanga), peeled and grated
- 1 cup orange juice or bitter orange juice
- 1 onion, finely chopped
- 3 cloves garlic, minced
- 1 teaspoon grated fresh ginger
- 1 tablespoon tomato paste
- 1 tablespoon soy sauce
- 1 tablespoon brown sugar
- 1 tablespoon vegetable oil
- 1 teaspoon salt (or to taste)
- 1/2 teaspoon black pepper
- 1/2 teaspoon cayenne pepper (adjust to your spice preference)
- 1 cup chicken broth
- 2 boiled eggs (optional, for garnish)
- Fresh parsley or cilantro for garnish

Instructions:

Marinate the Chicken:
- In a large bowl, combine the chicken pieces with the minced garlic, grated ginger, soy sauce, salt, black pepper, and cayenne pepper. Let it marinate for at least 1 hour, or overnight for best results.

Prepare the Pomtayer:
- Peel and grate the pomtayer. You can use a food processor for this step.

Preheat Oven:
- Preheat your oven to 350°F (175°C).

Cook the Chicken:
- Heat vegetable oil in a large oven-safe pot. Add chopped onions and cook until they become translucent. Add the marinated chicken and brown on all sides.
- Stir in tomato paste, brown sugar, and orange juice. Simmer for a few minutes.

Layer with Pomtayer:
- Mix the grated pomtayer with the chicken broth. Layer this mixture over the chicken in the pot.

Bake:
- Cover the pot and place it in the preheated oven. Bake for about 1.5 to 2 hours or until the pomtayer is tender and the flavors have melded. You may want to uncover it for the last 20-30 minutes to allow the top to brown.

Serve:
- Garnish with boiled eggs (sliced) and fresh parsley or cilantro.

Enjoy your delicious Surinamese Pom! This dish is often served with rice or bread to soak up the flavorful juices.

**Peruvian Anticuchos**

Ingredients:

- 1.5 to 2 lbs beef heart, cleaned and cut into bite-sized pieces
- 1/4 cup aji panca paste (Peruvian red chili pepper paste)
- 3 cloves garlic, minced
- 1 teaspoon ground cumin
- 1 teaspoon dried oregano
- Salt and pepper to taste
- 1/4 cup red wine vinegar
- 1/4 cup vegetable oil
- Wooden skewers, soaked in water for at least 30 minutes

Instructions:

Prepare the Marinade:
- In a bowl, combine aji panca paste, minced garlic, ground cumin, dried oregano, salt, pepper, red wine vinegar, and vegetable oil. Mix well to form a marinade.

Marinate the Beef Heart:
- Place the beef heart pieces in a large dish or a resealable plastic bag. Pour the marinade over the meat, ensuring each piece is well coated. Marinate for at least 4 hours or overnight in the refrigerator.

Skewering:
- Preheat your grill or barbecue.
- Thread the marinated beef heart pieces onto the soaked wooden skewers.

Grill:
- Grill the skewers over medium-high heat, turning occasionally, until the meat is cooked to your desired doneness. The edges should be slightly charred for authentic flavor.

Serve:
- Serve the Anticuchos hot, traditionally with a side of boiled potatoes or corn on the cob. Some people also enjoy them with a drizzle of aji verde sauce (green chili sauce).

Peruvian Anticuchos are not only flavorful but also represent the country's diverse culinary heritage. Adjust the spice level according to your preference and enjoy this delicious Peruvian street food!

## Brazillian Quindim

Ingredients:

- 1 cup unsalted butter, softened
- 2 cups granulated sugar
- 2 cups sweetened shredded coconut
- 2 cups fresh coconut milk or canned coconut milk
- 1 cup egg yolks (approximately 18-20 large egg yolks)
- 1 teaspoon vanilla extract
- Pinch of salt

Instructions:

Preheat Oven:
- Preheat your oven to 350°F (175°C). Grease and flour a muffin tin or individual quindim molds.

Prepare Ingredients:
- Separate egg yolks from whites, making sure there are no traces of egg whites in the yolks.

Combine Butter and Sugar:
- In a large bowl, cream together the softened butter and granulated sugar until light and fluffy.

Add Coconut:
- Add the sweetened shredded coconut to the butter and sugar mixture. Mix well.

Mix in Egg Yolks:
- Gradually add the egg yolks to the mixture, one at a time, mixing well after each addition.

Add Vanilla and Coconut Milk:
- Stir in the vanilla extract and slowly add the coconut milk to the batter, mixing until well combined. The mixture should have a smooth and slightly thick consistency.

Assemble Quindim:
- Pour the batter into the prepared muffin tin or molds, filling them about three-quarters full.

Bake:
- Place the molds in a water bath (bain-marie) and bake in the preheated oven for approximately 30-40 minutes or until the tops are golden and a toothpick inserted into the center comes out clean

Cool:
- Allow the Quindim to cool in the molds for a few minutes before transferring them to a wire rack to cool completely.

Serve:
- Once cooled, refrigerate the Quindim for a few hours before serving. This dessert is typically served chilled.

Enjoy these golden, sweet treats with their rich coconut flavor and smooth texture. Quindim is often enjoyed at celebrations and festive occasions in Brazil.

**Colombian Cazuela de Mariscos**

Ingredients:

- 1 lb mixed seafood (shrimp, mussels, squid, fish fillets, etc.)
- 1 onion, finely chopped
- 2 tomatoes, diced
- 1 bell pepper, diced
- 3 cloves garlic, minced
- 1/4 cup cilantro, chopped
- 1/4 cup green onions, chopped
- 1/4 cup achiote oil (annatto oil) for color (optional)
- 4 cups fish or seafood broth
- 1 cup coconut milk
- 1 teaspoon ground cumin
- 1 teaspoon paprika
- Salt and pepper to taste
- Lime wedges for serving

Instructions:

Prepare Seafood:
- Clean and devein shrimp. If using mussels, clean and debeard them. Cut squid into rings, and dice fish fillets into bite-sized pieces.

Make Achiote Oil (Optional):
- If you're using achiote oil for color, heat a small amount of oil with achiote seeds until the oil takes on a reddish color. Strain out the seeds.

Sauté Vegetables:
- In a large pot, heat achiote oil or regular oil over medium heat. Sauté onions, tomatoes, bell pepper, and garlic until softened.

Add Broth and Coconut Milk:
- Pour in the fish or seafood broth and coconut milk. Bring to a simmer.

Season the Broth:
- Add ground cumin, paprika, salt, and pepper to the broth. Adjust the seasoning to your taste.

Add Seafood:
- Add the mixed seafood to the simmering broth. Cook until the seafood is just cooked through, ensuring not to overcook.

Finish with Herbs:

- Stir in chopped cilantro and green onions. Let it simmer for a few more minutes.

Serve:
- Ladle the Cazuela de Mariscos into bowls. Serve with lime wedges on the side.

Enjoy your Colombian Cazuela de Mariscos, a comforting and flavorful seafood stew that showcases the diverse and delicious seafood available in Colombian coastal regions.

**Uruguayan Morcilla Dulce**

Ingredients:

- 1 lb pig's blood
- 1 cup rice
- 1 onion, finely chopped
- 1/2 cup sugar
- 1/4 cup honey
- 1 teaspoon ground cinnamon
- 1/2 teaspoon ground cloves
- 1/2 teaspoon ground nutmeg
- Salt and pepper to taste
- Hog casings (for stuffing)

Instructions:

Prepare Rice:
- Cook the rice according to package instructions until it's slightly undercooked.

Prepare Casings:
- Rinse and soak hog casings in water, following the instructions on the packaging.

Prepare Blood:
- In a large bowl, mix pig's blood with sugar, honey, ground cinnamon, ground cloves, ground nutmeg, salt, and pepper. Stir until the sugar is dissolved.

Combine Ingredients:
- Add the slightly undercooked rice and finely chopped onion to the blood mixture. Mix well until everything is thoroughly combined.

Stuff the Casings:
- Using a sausage stuffer or a funnel, fill the hog casings with the Morcilla Dulce mixture. Tie off the ends of the sausages.

Cooking:
- Bring a pot of water to a gentle simmer. Add the Morcilla Dulce sausages and simmer for about 30-40 minutes.

Cooling:
- After simmering, allow the sausages to cool. You can store them in the refrigerator for a day to allow the flavors to meld.

Serve:

- Morcilla Dulce can be served in various ways – grilled, pan-fried, or even sliced and added to stews or other dishes.

Remember that recipes for Morcilla Dulce can vary from region to region and from one family to another. Adjust the seasoning and sweetness to your liking, and enjoy this unique and flavorful Uruguayan blood sausage.

**Chilean Pebre**

Ingredients:

- 2 medium-sized tomatoes, diced
- 1 small red onion, finely chopped
- 1/2 cup fresh cilantro, finely chopped
- 1/4 cup fresh parsley, finely chopped
- 1-2 cloves garlic, minced
- 1-2 green chili peppers (such as jalapeños), finely chopped
- 3 tablespoons red wine vinegar
- 2 tablespoons olive oil
- Salt and pepper to taste

Instructions:

Prepare Vegetables:
- Dice the tomatoes, finely chop the red onion, cilantro, and parsley. Mince the garlic, and finely chop the green chili peppers. Place everything in a bowl.

Mix Ingredients:
- In the bowl with the vegetables, add red wine vinegar and olive oil. Mix everything together until well combined.

Season:
- Season the Pebre with salt and pepper according to your taste. Start with a small amount and adjust as needed.

Let It Rest:
- Allow the Pebre to sit for at least 15-30 minutes before serving. This allows the flavors to meld and develop.

Serve:
- Pebre is often served as a condiment alongside grilled meats, empanadas, or as a topping for bread. It adds a fresh and zesty kick to various dishes.

Chilean Pebre is versatile, and the ingredients and quantities can be adjusted based on personal preferences. Some variations might include the addition of a small amount of chopped bell peppers, a pinch of cumin, or a squeeze of lime juice. Feel free to experiment and tailor the recipe to suit your taste.

**Paraguayan Mbeju**

Ingredients:

- 2 cups cassava (yuca) starch
- 1 1/2 cups grated cheese (commonly queso Paraguay or queso fresco)
- 1/2 cup unsalted butter, softened
- 1/2 cup whole milk
- 1/2 teaspoon salt (or to taste)

Instructions:

Prepare Cassava Starch:
- In a large mixing bowl, place the cassava starch.

Add Cheese:
- Add the grated cheese to the cassava starch.

Incorporate Butter:
- Add the softened butter to the mixture. Use your hands to incorporate the butter evenly into the dry ingredients.

Mix in Milk:
- Gradually add the milk to the mixture, kneading the dough as you go. Continue kneading until you have a smooth, uniform dough. The consistency should be firm but pliable.

Season:
- Add salt to the dough and knead it in to ensure even distribution. Taste and adjust the salt as needed.

Form Dough Balls:
- Divide the dough into golf ball-sized portions and shape them into balls.

Flatten and Cook:
- Place a dough ball between two sheets of parchment paper or plastic wrap. Flatten it into a thin disc, about 1/4 inch thick.
- Heat a griddle or non-stick skillet over medium heat. Cook the Mbeju on each side until golden brown and cooked through, about 2-3 minutes per side.

Serve:
- Serve Mbeju warm as a snack, breakfast item, or accompaniment to other dishes.

Mbeju is known for its unique texture and cheesy flavor, making it a favorite among Paraguayans. You can enjoy it on its own or pair it with coffee, tea, or other beverages.

**Ecuadorian Llapingachos**

Ingredients:

For the Potato Patties:

- 4 large potatoes, peeled and boiled
- 1 cup queso fresco or farmer's cheese, grated
- Salt to taste

For the Filling:

- 1 cup cooked and finely chopped chorizo or beef
- 1/2 cup onion, finely chopped
- 1/4 cup bell pepper, finely chopped
- 1 tablespoon vegetable oil
- Salt and pepper to taste

For Serving:

- Aji sauce (optional, for serving)

Instructions:

1. Prepare the Potato Patties:

    Boil the potatoes until they are fork-tender. Drain and let them cool slightly.
    Mash the boiled potatoes in a large bowl until smooth.
    Add the grated queso fresco or farmer's cheese to the mashed potatoes and season with salt. Mix well to combine.

2. Make the Filling:

    In a skillet, heat vegetable oil over medium heat.
    Add chopped onion and bell pepper to the skillet and sauté until softened.
    Add the cooked and chopped chorizo or beef to the skillet. Season with salt and pepper. Cook until everything is well combined and heated through.

3. Assemble Llapingachos:

Take a portion of the mashed potato mixture and flatten it into a disk in the palm of your hand.
Place a spoonful of the chorizo or beef filling in the center of the potato disk.
Fold the edges of the potato over the filling, shaping it into a stuffed patty. Seal the edges well.

4. Cook Llapingachos:

    Heat a pan or griddle over medium heat.
    Cook the llapingachos on both sides until they are golden brown and have a crispy exterior.

5. Serve:

    Serve llapingachos hot as a side dish, typically alongside grilled meats.
    Optionally, serve with aji sauce for extra flavor.

Llapingachos are a delightful and savory addition to Ecuadorian meals, and their cheesy potato goodness makes them a favorite among locals and visitors alike.

**Venezuelan Tequeños**

Ingredients:

For the Dough:

- 2 cups all-purpose flour
- 1/2 teaspoon salt
- 1 tablespoon sugar
- 1/2 cup unsalted butter, cold and cut into small cubes
- 1/2 cup water (approximate)

For the Filling:

- Queso blanco (white cheese), such as queso de mano or queso fresco, cut into sticks (about 3-4 inches long and 1/2 inch wide)
- Alternatively, you can use mozzarella or another stretchy cheese

For Frying:

- Vegetable oil for deep-frying

Instructions:

1. Prepare the Dough:

    In a large bowl, combine the flour, salt, and sugar.
    Add the cold, cubed butter to the flour mixture. Use your fingers or a pastry cutter to cut the butter into the flour until it resembles coarse crumbs.
    Gradually add water, a little at a time, and knead until the dough comes together.
    The dough should be smooth and not too sticky. Add more water or flour if needed.
    Wrap the dough in plastic wrap and refrigerate for at least 30 minutes.

2. Assemble the Tequeños:

    Preheat the oil in a deep fryer or a deep, heavy-bottomed pan to 350°F (175°C).
    Roll out the chilled dough on a floured surface into a thin rectangle.
    Cut the dough into strips, about 3-4 inches wide.
    Place a cheese stick at one end of a dough strip and roll it up, sealing the edge with a little water. Repeat for the remaining dough and cheese sticks.

3. Fry the Tequeños:

   Carefully place the tequeños in the hot oil and fry until they are golden brown and crispy, usually for about 3-4 minutes.
   Remove the tequeños with a slotted spoon and place them on a paper towel-lined plate to absorb any excess oil.

4. Serve:

   Serve the tequeños warm, either on their own or with a dipping sauce like guasacaca (avocado salsa) or sweet chili sauce.

Enjoy these delicious Venezuelan tequeños as a tasty snack or appetizer at your next gathering!

**Bolivian Api**

Ingredients:

- 2 cups purple corn flour (harina de maíz morado)
- 8 cups water
- 1 to 1 1/2 cups sugar (adjust to taste)
- 1 cinnamon stick
- 4 whole cloves
- 1 orange or lemon peel (optional)
- 1 teaspoon vanilla extract (optional)
- Ground cinnamon for garnish

Instructions:

1. Prepare the Purple Corn Mixture:

> In a large pot, mix the purple corn flour with 4 cups of water, stirring to dissolve any lumps.
> Strain the mixture into the pot, using a fine mesh strainer or cheesecloth to remove any remaining lumps.

2. Cook the Purple Corn Mixture:

> Add the cinnamon stick, cloves, and orange or lemon peel (if using) to the strained purple corn mixture.
> Place the pot over medium heat and bring the mixture to a simmer. Reduce the heat to low and let it simmer for about 30-40 minutes, stirring occasionally.

3. Sweeten the Api:

> Add sugar to the pot, starting with 1 cup. Adjust the sweetness to your liking by adding more sugar if needed. Stir well to dissolve the sugar.
> Continue simmering the mixture for an additional 10-15 minutes, allowing the flavors to meld.

4. Add Vanilla Extract (Optional):

> If using vanilla extract, add it to the pot and stir well.

5. Strain and Serve:

   Strain the Api again to remove any solids, using a fine mesh strainer or cheesecloth. Discard the spices and any remaining solids.

6. Serve:

   Pour the strained Api into mugs or cups.
   Garnish each serving with a sprinkle of ground cinnamon on top.
   Serve the Bolivian Api warm and enjoy its sweet and spiced flavors.

Bolivian Api is often enjoyed with pastries or bread. It's a traditional and comforting beverage that reflects the unique flavors and ingredients of Bolivian cuisine.

**Guyanese Cook-up Rice**

Ingredients:

- 2 cups rice (preferably parboiled rice)
- 1 lb meat of choice (chicken, beef, or pork), cut into bite-sized pieces
- 1 cup coconut milk
- 1 cup cooked peas (black-eyed peas or red beans)
- 1 large onion, chopped
- 2 cloves garlic, minced
- 1 bell pepper, chopped
- 1 large tomato, chopped
- 2 sprigs fresh thyme
- 2 tablespoons vegetable oil
- 2 cups water
- Salt and pepper to taste

Instructions:

1. Prepare the Meat:

    Season the meat with salt and pepper.
    In a large pot or Dutch oven, heat the vegetable oil over medium heat. Brown the meat on all sides.

2. Add Aromatics:

    Add the chopped onion, minced garlic, and bell pepper to the pot. Sauté until the vegetables are softened.
    Stir in the chopped tomato and fresh thyme. Cook for an additional 2-3 minutes.

3. Add Rice and Coconut Milk:

    Add the rice to the pot, stirring to coat it in the flavorful mixture.
    Pour in the coconut milk and water. Stir well.

4. Incorporate Cooked Peas:

    Add the pre-cooked peas (black-eyed peas or red beans) to the pot.

5. Simmer:

   Bring the mixture to a boil, then reduce the heat to low. Cover the pot and let it simmer for about 25-30 minutes or until the rice is cooked and the liquid is absorbed.

6. Check and Adjust Seasoning:

   Check the seasoning and adjust with salt and pepper as needed.

7. Serve:

   Once the rice is fully cooked and the flavors have melded, fluff the rice with a fork. Serve Guyanese Cook-up Rice hot, either as a standalone dish or with your favorite side.

Enjoy this hearty and flavorful dish that captures the essence of Guyanese cuisine. The combination of coconut milk, aromatic spices, and various meats makes Guyanese Cook-up Rice a delightful and satisfying meal.

**Colombian Arroz con Coco**

Ingredients:

- 2 cups long-grain white rice
- 2 cups coconut milk
- 1 cup water
- 1 cup shredded coconut (unsweetened)
- 2 tablespoons vegetable oil
- 1 teaspoon salt
- 1/2 cup raisins (optional, for added sweetness)
- Fresh cilantro or parsley for garnish (optional)

Instructions:

1. Rinse and Soak Rice:

    Rinse the rice under cold water until the water runs clear.
    Soak the rinsed rice in water for about 15-20 minutes. Drain the rice.

2. Toast Shredded Coconut:

    In a dry pan over medium heat, toast the shredded coconut until it turns golden brown. Stir frequently to prevent burning. Set aside.

3. Cook the Rice:

    In a large pot, heat the vegetable oil over medium heat.
    Add the soaked and drained rice to the pot. Stir and cook for a couple of minutes until the rice grains are well-coated with the oil.
    Pour in the coconut milk and water. Add salt and stir well.
    Bring the mixture to a boil, then reduce the heat to low. Cover the pot with a tight-fitting lid and simmer for about 15-20 minutes or until the rice is cooked and the liquid is absorbed.

4. Add Shredded Coconut and Raisins:

    Once the rice is cooked, gently fold in the toasted shredded coconut and raisins, if using.
    Cover the pot and let it sit for a few more minutes, allowing the flavors to meld.

5. Serve:

    Fluff the rice with a fork and transfer it to a serving dish.
    Garnish with fresh cilantro or parsley, if desired.

6. Enjoy:

Serve Colombian Arroz con Coco as a flavorful and aromatic side dish, particularly complementing dishes with a tropical or seafood theme.

This dish offers a delightful combination of coconut flavors and a slightly sweet touch from the raisins, making it a unique and tasty addition to your Colombian culinary repertoire.

**Argentinian Provoleta**

Ingredients:

- 1 lb provolone cheese, sliced (about 1/2 inch thick)
- 2 tablespoons olive oil
- 2 cloves garlic, minced
- 1 teaspoon dried oregano
- 1 teaspoon crushed red pepper flakes (optional)
- Black pepper to taste
- Fresh oregano or parsley for garnish
- Sliced tomatoes or roasted red peppers (optional, for serving)
- Crusty bread, for serving

Instructions:

1. Prepare the Cheese:

    Preheat the oven to 400°F (200°C).
    Slice the provolone cheese into rounds, about 1/2 inch thick.

2. Season the Cheese:

    In a skillet, heat the olive oil over medium heat. Add the minced garlic and sauté for about 1 minute until fragrant.
    Place the provolone slices in the skillet, arranging them in a single layer.
    Sprinkle dried oregano, crushed red pepper flakes (if using), and black pepper over the cheese.

3. Bake the Provoleta:

    Transfer the skillet to the preheated oven and bake for about 10-15 minutes, or until the cheese is melted and bubbly. Keep an eye on it to avoid overcooking.

4. Garnish and Serve:

    Once out of the oven, garnish the Provoleta with fresh oregano or parsley.
    Serve the Provoleta hot, directly from the skillet. Optionally, accompany it with sliced tomatoes or roasted red peppers.
    Provide crusty bread for dipping and spreading the melted cheese.

5. Enjoy:

Dig into the gooey, melted goodness of Argentinian Provoleta, savoring the seasoned provolone with the aromatic blend of herbs and spices.

Provoleta is not only a delicious appetizer but also a social and shareable dish, perfect for enjoying with friends and family.

**Chilean Humitas en Olla**

Ingredients:

For the Dough:

- 6 fresh ears of corn
- 1 cup cornmeal
- 1/2 cup all-purpose flour
- 1/2 cup vegetable oil
- 1 teaspoon baking powder
- Salt to taste

For the Filling:

- 1 large onion, finely chopped
- 2 tablespoons vegetable oil
- 1 teaspoon paprika
- 1 teaspoon ground cumin
- Salt and pepper to taste
- 1/2 cup black olives, chopped (optional)

For Assembly:

- Corn husks, soaked in warm water for at least 1 hour

Instructions:

1. Prepare the Corn:

    Shuck the fresh corn and carefully remove the kernels from the cobs.
    Grind or process half of the corn kernels in a blender or food processor until you get a coarse paste.
    Mix the coarse paste with the remaining whole corn kernels in a large bowl.

2. Make the Dough:

    In the bowl with the corn mixture, add cornmeal, all-purpose flour, vegetable oil, baking powder, and salt. Mix well until you have a thick, homogeneous dough.

3. Prepare the Filling:

- In a skillet, heat vegetable oil over medium heat. Add finely chopped onions and sauté until translucent.
- Add paprika, ground cumin, salt, and pepper to the onions. Cook for an additional 2-3 minutes until the spices are fragrant.
- Mix the spiced onions with the corn dough. Add chopped black olives if desired. Adjust the seasoning to taste.

4. Assemble the Humitas:

- Take a soaked corn husk, place a generous spoonful of the corn dough mixture in the center, and fold the sides to form a rectangular package. Fold the bottom and top to enclose the filling completely.
- Tie the humita with a thin strip of corn husk to secure it.

5. Steam the Humitas:

- Arrange the humitas in a large pot fitted with a steaming basket.
- Steam the humitas over simmering water for about 45-60 minutes or until the dough is cooked through and has a firm consistency.

6. Serve:

- Allow the humitas to cool slightly before serving.
- Humitas en Olla are typically served warm, enjoyed as a main dish or snack.

Chilean Humitas en Olla are a delightful representation of traditional Chilean cuisine, capturing the flavors of fresh corn and savory spices.

## Ecuadorian Bolón de Verde

Ingredients:

- 4 large green plantains
- 1 cup queso fresco (fresh cheese), crumbled
- 1 cup chicharrón (fried pork belly or pork rinds), finely chopped (optional)
- 1/4 cup green onions, finely chopped
- 1/4 cup cilantro, finely chopped
- Salt to taste
- Vegetable oil for frying

Instructions:

1. Prepare the Green Plantains:

   Peel the green plantains by cutting off the ends and making a shallow incision along the length of each plantain. Peel away the skin.
   Cut the plantains into chunks, about 2 inches in length.

2. Boil the Plantains:

   In a large pot, bring water to a boil. Add the plantain chunks and a pinch of salt.
   Boil the plantains for about 15-20 minutes or until they are fork-tender.
   Drain the plantains and let them cool slightly.

3. Mash the Plantains:

   Place the boiled plantains in a large bowl. Use a potato masher or the back of a fork to mash the plantains until you have a smooth, dough-like consistency.
   Add salt to taste and mix well.

4. Assemble the Bolones:

   Take a portion of the mashed plantains and flatten it in the palm of your hand.
   Place a spoonful of crumbled queso fresco and chopped chicharrón in the center.
   Fold the plantain mixture around the filling, shaping it into a ball. Ensure that the filling is completely enclosed.

5. Fry the Bolones:

In a deep skillet or frying pan, heat vegetable oil over medium heat.
Carefully place the bolones in the hot oil and fry until they are golden brown on all sides. This usually takes about 5-7 minutes.
Use a slotted spoon to remove the bolones from the oil and place them on a plate lined with paper towels to absorb any excess oil.

6. Serve:

Garnish the bolones with chopped green onions and cilantro.
Serve the bolones warm and enjoy them with additional toppings like aji (hot sauce) or avocado.

Bolón de Verde is a delicious and satisfying Ecuadorian snack that showcases the versatility of green plantains. The combination of the savory plantain dough with the cheese and chicharrón filling creates a delightful culinary experience.

**Bolivian Llajwa**

Ingredients:

- 4 medium tomatoes, finely chopped
- 2-4 hot peppers (locoto or other hot chili peppers), finely chopped (adjust according to your spice preference)
- 1 small red onion, finely chopped
- 1 bunch of cilantro, finely chopped
- 2 cloves garlic, minced
- 1 tablespoon lime or lemon juice
- Salt to taste

Instructions:

Prepare Ingredients:
- Finely chop the tomatoes, hot peppers, red onion, and cilantro. Mince the garlic.

Combine Ingredients:
- In a bowl, combine the chopped tomatoes, hot peppers, red onion, cilantro, and minced garlic.

Add Citrus Juice:
- Squeeze lime or lemon juice over the mixture. Adjust the amount to your liking.

Season with Salt:
- Add salt to taste. Start with a small amount and adjust as needed.

Mix Well:
- Mix all the ingredients thoroughly to ensure an even distribution of flavors.

Let it Rest:
- Allow the llajwa to sit for at least 15-30 minutes before serving. This helps the flavors meld.

Serve:
- Llajwa is ready to be served! It can be served in a small bowl or used as a topping for various dishes.

Llajwa is known for its spicy kick and fresh, vibrant flavors. It adds a delightful element to Bolivian cuisine, enhancing the taste of many dishes. Adjust the heat level by adding more or fewer hot peppers according to your preference. Enjoy it with empanadas, grilled meats, or any dish you'd like to spice up!

**Uruguayan Revuelto Gramajo**

Ingredients:

- 4 large potatoes, peeled and cut into thin matchsticks (French fries)
- 6 large eggs
- 100g cooked ham, diced
- 1/2 cup frozen green peas (optional)
- 1/2 cup vegetable oil (for frying the potatoes)
- Salt and pepper to taste
- Chopped parsley for garnish (optional)

Instructions:

1. Prepare the French Fries:

    Heat the vegetable oil in a deep fryer or a large skillet over medium-high heat. Fry the potato matchsticks until golden brown and crispy. Remove them from the oil and place them on a paper towel to drain excess oil. Sprinkle with salt.

2. Cook the Eggs:

    In a bowl, crack the eggs and whisk them until well beaten. Season with salt and pepper.
    Heat a non-stick skillet over medium heat. Pour the beaten eggs into the skillet. As the eggs start to set, gently scramble them with a spatula. Continue to cook until the eggs are mostly set but still slightly runny.
    Add the diced ham and green peas (if using) to the eggs. Continue to scramble until the eggs are fully cooked and the ingredients are well combined.

3. Assemble Revuelto Gramajo:

    Add the crispy French fries to the scrambled eggs mixture. Toss everything together until the fries are evenly distributed.

4. Serve:

    Transfer the Revuelto Gramajo to a serving dish.
    Garnish with chopped parsley if desired.
    Serve the dish hot, either on its own or with a side of crusty bread.

Revuelto Gramajo is a delicious and comforting dish that combines the textures of crispy fries with the savory goodness of scrambled eggs. It's a popular choice for a hearty breakfast or brunch in Uruguay.

**Peruvian Aji de Gallina**

Ingredients:

- 1.5 lbs boneless, skinless chicken breasts or thighs, cooked and shredded
- 2 cups chicken broth (from cooking the chicken)
- 2 tablespoons vegetable oil
- 1 large onion, finely chopped
- 4 cloves garlic, minced
- 2 aji amarillo peppers, seeds removed and finely chopped (or aji amarillo paste)
- 1 cup walnuts, finely ground
- 1 cup evaporated milk
- 1 cup grated Parmesan cheese
- Salt and pepper to taste
- 4-6 boiled potatoes, sliced
- Cooked rice for serving
- Hard-boiled eggs and black olives for garnish

Instructions:

1. Cook and Shred the Chicken:

   In a pot, cook the chicken in salted water until fully cooked. Shred the chicken and set aside, reserving 2 cups of the chicken broth.

2. Prepare the Aji Amarillo Sauce:

   In a blender, combine the aji amarillo peppers (or paste) with the walnuts and a portion of the chicken broth. Blend until you have a smooth, orange-colored sauce.

3. Cook the Aji de Gallina:

   In a large pan, heat vegetable oil over medium heat. Add chopped onions and minced garlic. Sauté until the onions are soft and translucent.
   Add the aji amarillo and walnut sauce to the pan. Cook for a few minutes, stirring constantly.
   Incorporate the shredded chicken into the sauce, mixing well to coat the chicken. Pour in the remaining chicken broth, evaporated milk, and grated Parmesan cheese. Stir and let it simmer until the sauce thickens.

Season with salt and pepper to taste. Adjust the spiciness by adding more aji amarillo if desired.

4. Serve:

Serve the Aji de Gallina over a bed of rice and sliced boiled potatoes.
Garnish with hard-boiled eggs and black olives.
Optionally, sprinkle additional grated Parmesan cheese on top.

Enjoy this flavorful and creamy Peruvian dish that combines the unique heat of aji amarillo peppers with the richness of walnuts and cheese.

## Brazilian Brigadeiro

Ingredients:

- 1 can (14 ounces) sweetened condensed milk
- 2 tablespoons unsweetened cocoa powder
- 2 tablespoons unsalted butter
- A pinch of salt
- Chocolate sprinkles (traditional) or other coatings like shredded coconut or finely chopped nuts

Instructions:

1. Prepare the Mixture:

    In a non-stick pan, combine the sweetened condensed milk, cocoa powder, butter, and a pinch of salt.
    Cook the mixture over medium heat, stirring constantly to prevent burning. Use a spatula to scrape the sides and bottom of the pan.
    Continue cooking and stirring until the mixture thickens and starts to pull away from the sides of the pan. It should have a fudgy consistency.

2. Chill the Mixture:

    Remove the pan from heat and let the mixture cool to room temperature.
    Once cooled, refrigerate the mixture for at least 1-2 hours or until it is firm enough to handle.

3. Shape into Balls:

    Grease your hands with butter to prevent sticking. Take small portions of the mixture and roll them into small balls, about the size of a cherry.
    Place the chocolate sprinkles (or your preferred coating) in a bowl.
    Roll each Brigadeiro ball in the sprinkles, coating them evenly.

4. Serve:

    Place the Brigadeiros in small paper cups or arrange them on a plate.
    Serve and enjoy these delightful Brazilian chocolate truffles!

Brigadeiros are not only delicious but also a fun and festive treat. You can experiment with different coatings or even add a surprise in the center, like a chocolate or nut. They make for a wonderful addition to any celebration or as a sweet indulgence for chocolate lovers.

www.ingramcontent.com/pod-product-compliance
Lightning Source LLC
LaVergne TN
LVHW081605060526
838201LV00054B/2082